ORIGAMI
DINOSAURS

YOSHIHIDE MOMOTA

KODANSHA INTERNATIONAL
New York • Tokyo • London

Kodansha America, Inc.
114 Fifth Avenue, New York, New York 10011, U.S.A.

Kodansha International Ltd.
17-14 Otowa 1-chome, Bunkyo-ku, Tokyo 112, Japan

Published in 1993 by Kodansha America, Inc.

The publisher wishes to acknowledge the participation of Mark Kennedy
of the Friends of the Origami Center of America, who adapted
instructions for the American reader. Thanks are also extended to Mark
Norell, a paleontologist at the American Museum of Natural History,
who insured that descriptions of the dinosaurs were in keeping with the
latest findings in the field.

Printed in the United States of America

93 94 95 96   6 5 4 3 2 1

Library of Congress Cataloging-in-Publication Data

    Momotani, Yoshihide
        Origami dinosaurs / Yoshihide Momotani.
            p. cm.
        Summary: Provides an introduction to the basics of origami
    and gives more detailed instructions for making fourteen dinosaurs
    out of folded paper.
        ISBN 1-56836-008-8
        1. Origami—Juvenile literature. 2. Dinosaurs in art—Juvenile
    literature. [1. Origami. 2. Dinosaurs in art. 3. Handicraft.]
    I. Title.
    TT870.M53   1993
    736'.982—dc20
                                        93-17643
                                          CIP
                                          AC

Book Design by Eric Baker Design Associates, Inc.
Photography by Eriko Momotani
Line Drawings by Miyuki Ozaki

COVER PHOTOGRAPH: Tyrannosaurus. Title Page: Tyrannosaurus, mother
and baby. PAGE 17: Godzilla, Stegosaurus. BACK COVER: baby dinosaurs.

The text of this book was set in Berkeley Oldstyle and Bureau Eagle

Printed and bound by Arcata Graphics, Kingsport, Tennessee

CONTENTS

INTRODUCTION

The dinosaurs presented here are the work of a biologist, but one with imagination. No one, after all, knows just what dinosaurs looked like; the color of a dinosaur's skin can only be guessed at. Artists have always based their drawings upon the data of paleontologists. Their evidence has been gathered from all over the world, including Japan. Some tracks of plant-eating dinosaurs have been discovered in Gumma Prefecture, while footprints of theropods, or meat-eating dinosaurs, have been found in Kumamoto Prefecture. The bones of Hadrosaurs (like the *Edmontosaurus* in this book) have been discovered in Tokushima Prefecture and in Kyushu.

The reader may notice that some of the names of dinosaurs they are familiar with have changed. This is because of new research. For example, the first *Apatosaurus* was discovered in 1877. Another specimen was discovered in 1879 and named the *Brontosaurus*. It has only been during the last twenty years that researchers have come to the conclusion that these dinosaurs were in fact the same species. In such a situation, the name used is always that given by the first discoverer—in this case, *Apatosaurus*.

Before making the models in this book, the reader should be sure to read the beginning of the book. Learning to fold the traditional Fish Base, Square Base, and Bird Base will serve as a good foundation for making many kinds of dinosaurs. After mastering these bases and learning how to make the models in this book, I hope you will experiment to create other species of dinosaurs, inventing forms that agree with your own research and the new information about dinosaurs that is continually being unearthed.

Modifying these models can be compared to making up music as you go along. By experimenting and playing around with form, type of paper, and size (see the baby *Tyrannosaurus* on the title page), new folders can express themselves in origami. Even if you are a beginner, by carefully following the diagrams and instructions in *Origami Dinosaurs* you will be able to make all kinds of prehistoric creatures, as well as science fiction's most famous monster, Godzilla.

All models in this book are the original creations of Yoshihide Momotani. Photography is by Eriko Momotani.

YOSHIHIDE MOMOTANI

BEFORE FOLDING

All of the models in this book are based upon a standard size of origami paper, 6 x 6 inches, which can be found easily in arts-and-crafts stores or can be cut to any square size. Before folding, make sure your hands are clean to avoid unwanted fingerprints.

First study the "Basic Folds & Symbols" section, which shows you how to read the language of the diagrams and how to make the basic folds. As you make each dinosaur, keep referring back to this section when you need to.

Folds should be made firmly—using the back of a fingernail helps. However, when you make a crease for landmark purposes only (to guide the eye and hand), make it as slight as possible. Your models will then be clean and bright.

When using the diagrams, you will discover that each one shows the result of the previous step as well as the action to be taken next. Keep looking ahead whenever you get stuck. Some people read words; others read pictures. Do whatever works best for you. If you carefully follow each step, one builds upon another, and the sequence of models is designed to introduce techniques gradually. However, the beginning folder may want to refer to the triangles on the contents page—a single triangle indicates the easiest model. Two triangles are Low-Intermediate Level, and three are High-Intermediate Level. Very young children will find it useful to fold along with their parents at first, and may want to begin with the Bird Base, quickly seeing results in the popular Crane (p. 14).

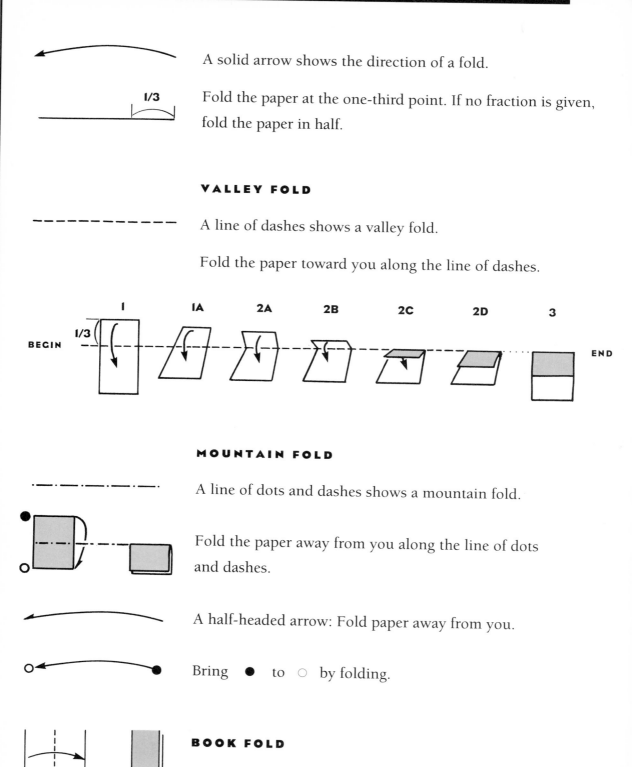

A solid arrow shows the direction of a fold.

Fold the paper at the one-third point. If no fraction is given, fold the paper in half.

VALLEY FOLD

A line of dashes shows a valley fold.

Fold the paper toward you along the line of dashes.

MOUNTAIN FOLD

A line of dots and dashes shows a mountain fold.

Fold the paper away from you along the line of dots and dashes.

A half-headed arrow: Fold paper away from you.

Bring ● to ○ by folding.

BOOK FOLD

Fold one edge to meet the opposite edge.

LANDMARK CREASE: A faint dotted line represents an already existing crease, or an already existing layer that is hidden by the paper. It is used as a point of reference.

Pull out from behind.

This symbol shows a fold that extends into a hidden part.

Press in here.

Pull.

Blow up here to create a three-dimensional shape.

Insert here.

Turn the paper over.

A swollen arrow shows that the following diagram is drawn to a larger scale. An arrow with a jagged tail means the opposite.

INSIDE REVERSE FOLD

Practice on a sample piece of paper.

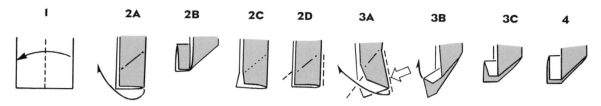

MAKING THE SHAPE

1 Valley fold thin strip of paper in half to the left.

MAKING A PRE-CREASE TO HELP

2A Mountain fold behind and to the left.

2B Unfold.

2C This is the crease you have made.

2D You will use the creases you have made to make the inside reverse fold.

The diagonal crease on the far side will change from a mountain into a valley fold. The folded edge of the sample paper will become a valley fold.

MAKING THE INSIDE REVERSE FOLD

3A Separate the two layers and push in on the folded edge, changing it from a mountain to a valley fold.

3B Continue pushing up.

3C Almost done—just flatten and sharpen.

COMPLETING THE INSIDE REVERSE FOLD

4 Completed

CRIMP (PLEAT):

A combination of mountain and valley folds that meet at one point. It is used to shift and shape paper.

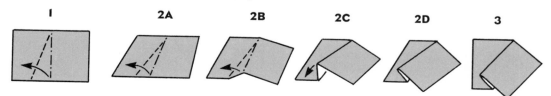

OUTSIDE REVERSE FOLD

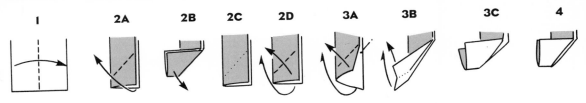

MAKING THE SHAPE

I Valley fold a thin strip of paper in half to the right.

MAKING A PRE-CREASE TO HELP

2A Valley fold to the left.

2B Unfold.

2C This is the crease you have made.

2D You will use the creases you have made to make the outside reverse fold.

On the lower layer the mountain fold will be changed to a valley fold.

MAKING THE OUTSIDE REVERSE FOLD

3A Separate the two layers and start to fold both to the left. The paper will pop slightly.

3B The paper has popped. Continue folding to the left.

3C Almost done—just flatten and sharpen.

COMPLETING THE OUTSIDE REVERSE FOLD

4 Completed.

SQUASH FOLD

Practice on a sample piece of paper.

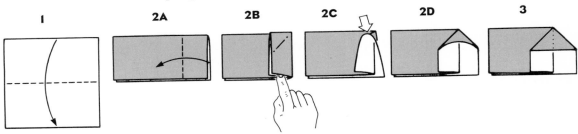

I Mountain fold paper in half.

2A Valley fold paper to the left.

2B Insert finger and open.

2C Push at point indicated.

2D Begin to flatten.

3 Completed.

FISH BASE

STEP 1

Valley fold side edges into the diagonal center crease.

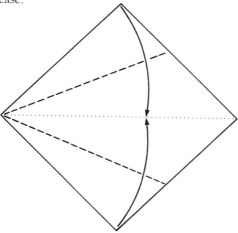

STEP 2

You now have the **Kite Base**. Mountain fold the tip of the kite behind so that it matches the top of the kite.

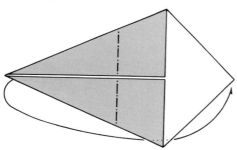

STEP 3

Insert finger into pocket and open up slightly. Bring raw edge to center line and flatten the former pocket.

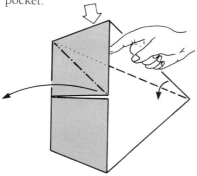

STEP 4

Repeat **Step 3** on the other side.

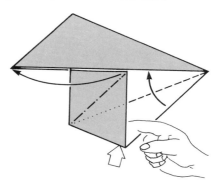

STEP 5

Lift top flap and valley fold to left.

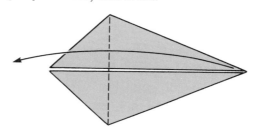

STEP 6

Turn over.

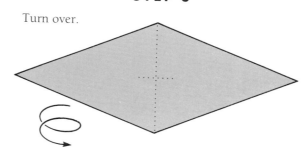

STEP 7

This is the traditional **Fish Base**. The *Apatosaurus, Anchisaurus, Allosaurus, Diplodocus, Edmontosaurus, Parasaurolophus,* and *Stegosaurus* models are made from this base.

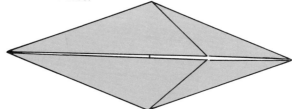

SQUARE BASE

(Also known as the **Preliminary Base**)

STEP 1

Place paper white side up. Bring one edge to the opposite edge.

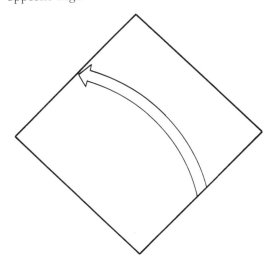

STEP 2

Hold edges firmly. Fold by sliding a finger while pressing.

STEP 3

Unfold.

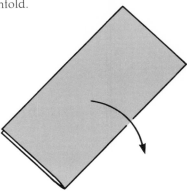

STEP 4

Repeat **Steps 1,2**, and **3** with the opposite edges.

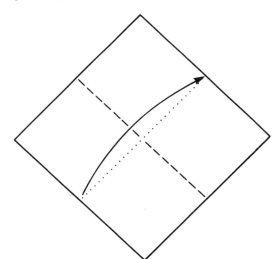

STEP 5

Unfold.

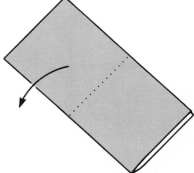

STEP 6

Mountain fold.

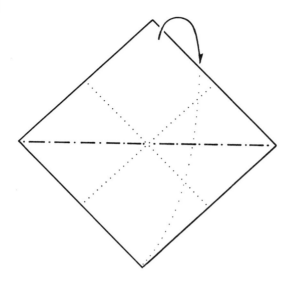

STEP 8

Bring ● to ○ and fold along the existing creases.

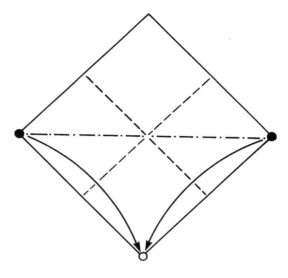

STEP 7

Unfold.

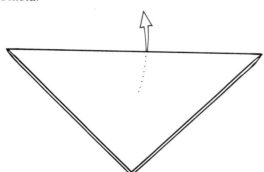

STEP 9

This is the traditional **Square Base**. The **Bird Base** is made from this base.

You can make many things from the **Square Base**. For example, make a **Square Base** with red paper and flip it over. You will see the classic origami flower.

BIRD BASE

STEP 1

Begin by making the **Square Base** (see p.11).

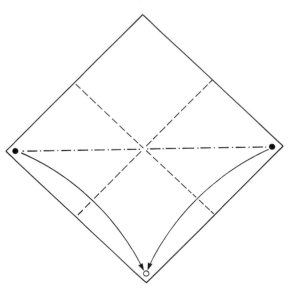

STEP 2

Lift the top layers and fold the double raw edges to the center. (Beginning folders may first mark the center with a landmark crease.)

STEP 3

(i) Fold the top down along the folded edges and unfold.(ii) Unfold triangular sections.

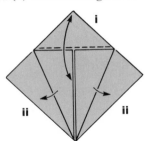

STEP 4

Lift up top layer and flatten.

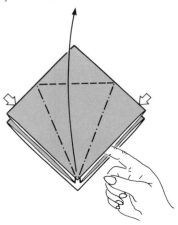

STEP 5

Repeat **Steps 2**, **3**, and **4**.

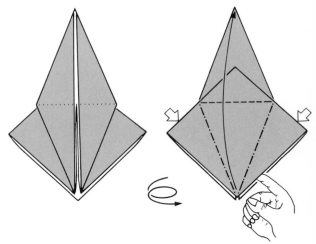

STEP 6

This is the traditional **Bird Base**. The *Rhamphorhyncus*, *Iguanodon*, *Godzilla*, and *Ornitholestes* models are made from this base. It is called the **Bird Base** because it is used to make the classic origami **Crane** (p.14).

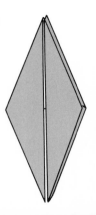

Almost everyone in Japan can make the origami **Crane**, symbol of good luck, long life, and health. If a child becomes seriously ill, classmates will come together to fold a thousand cranes in hopes of recovery.

STEP 1

Begin by making the **Bird Base** (p.13). Valley fold edges to center.

STEP 2

Turn over.

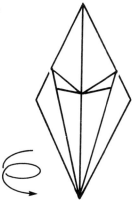

STEP 3

Repeat **Step 1**.

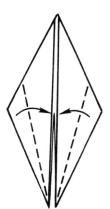

STEP 4

Inside reverse fold the neck and tail up.

STEP 5

Make a small inside reverse fold to form head. Fold wings down at right angles to body.

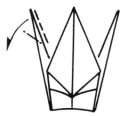

STEP 6

This is the classic **Crane**.

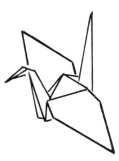

PRIMITIVE BASE

STEP 1

Place paper colored side up. Fold through **Step 8** of **Square Base** (p.12; paper is open). Turn over.

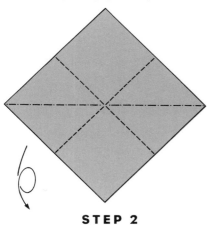

STEP 2

Fold and unfold side edges to center to make diagonal creases. Fold only as far as book folds. Turn over.

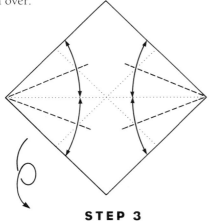

STEP 3

Bring ● to ○ and fold along the existing creases. (The next diagram is drawn to a larger scale.)

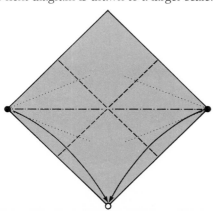

STEP 4

Fold down between the creases made in **Step 2** and unfold.

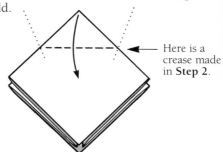

Here is a crease made in **Step 2**.

STEP 5

Bring the top corner to the crease at center.

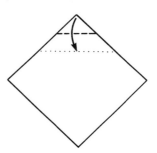

STEP 6

Fold over along crease.

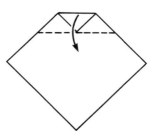

STEP 7

Turn over.

STEP 8

With bottom layer remaining on the table, open top layer so that it lies flat on the table. Squash both sides flat.

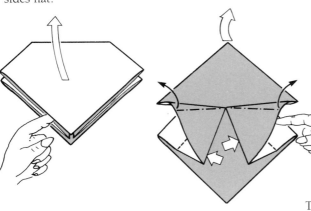

STEP 9

Inside reverse fold along the crease made by **Step 2**.

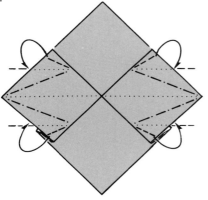

STEP 10

Valley fold model in half.

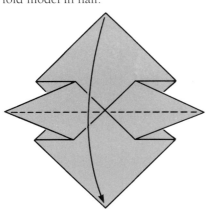

STEP 11

At the widest point, valley fold the top layer up.

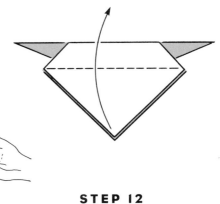

STEP 12

Turn over. Valley fold the top layer up.

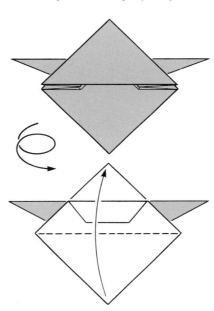

STEP 13

This is the **Primitive Base**, a new invention. It is used in making the **Dimetrodon** (see p.47).

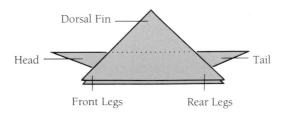

Dorsal Fin

Head   Tail

Front Legs   Rear Legs

GODZILLA

RHAMPHORHYNCUS

ANCHISAURUS

STEGOSAURUS

PARASAUROLOPHUS

ORNITHOLESTES

IGUANODON

APATOSAURUS

DINOSAURS

APATOSAURUS

FOLDED SIZE: 8 3/4"   **MATERIALS:** 2 sheets of 6" x 6" paper

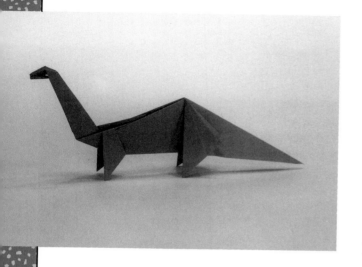

Recently the scientific name of the famous *Brontosaurus* has been changed to *Apatosaurus*. This gigantic dinosaur, which lived 140 million years ago, was more than twenty-five meters (eighty-two feet) long and weighed thirty tons. Based upon the shape and alignment of its teeth, it was most likely a plant-eater.

▼▼▼▼▼ HEAD & ▼▼▼▼▼ UPPER BODY SECTION

STEP 2

Valley fold side edges to center line.

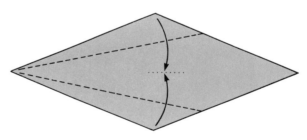

STEP 1

Starting with **Fish Base** shown on p.10, valley fold diagonally folded edges of flaps to vertical center crease.

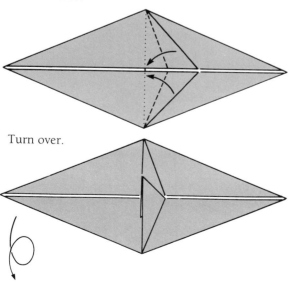

Turn over.

STEP 3

Valley fold model in half along center crease. Allow flaps formed in **Step 1** to swing free.

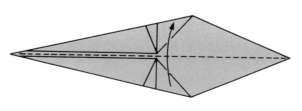

STEP 4

Starting between the legs (flaps), inside reverse fold the neck up.

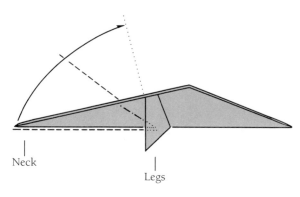

Neck

Legs

STEP 5

Starting 1/3 of the way down the back of the neck, inside reverse fold the head.

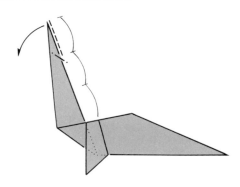

STEP 6

Outside reverse fold tip of head to touch front of neck. See close-up. **The Head and Upper Body Section** is now finished, and you are ready to make the **Body and Tail Section**.

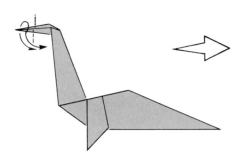

▾▾▾▾ BODY & TAIL ▾▾▾▾ SECTION

With second sheet of paper, repeat **Step 1** of **Head and Upper Body Section**.

▲▲▲▲▲▲▲▲▲▲▲▲▲▲▲▲▲▲▲▲▲▲▲▲▲▲▲▲▲.

STEP 7

Pull flap to left. Reverse valley fold to mountain fold along each leg and flatten.

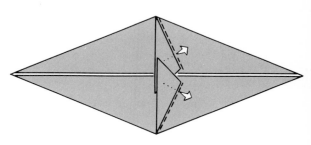

STEP 8

Mountain fold the tip behind so that it touches the center of the model.

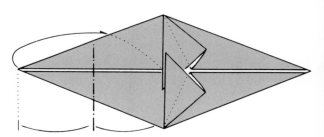

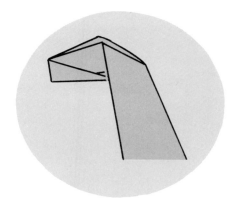

STEP 9

Mountain fold in half along center line, allowing legs to swing free.

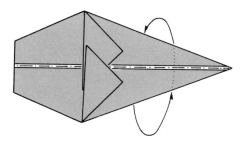

STEP 10

The **Body and Tail Section** is now finished, and you are ready to join the **Head and Upper Body Section** to it.

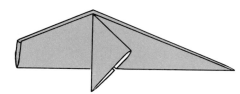

▼▼▼ JOINING THE ▼▼▼
TWO SECTIONS

STEP 11

Insert back tip of **Upper Body Section** into **Body and Tail Section** until **Body and Tail Section** slides under front legs.

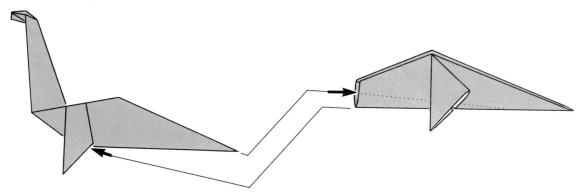

STEP 12

Open back legs out. Starting at highest point of dinosaur's back and ending at base, make a pleat to secure the two sections. (See *Crimp*, p. 8.) This lowers the tail.

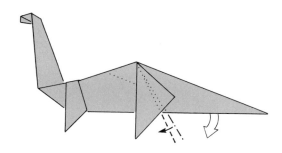

STEP 13

The model is now complete.

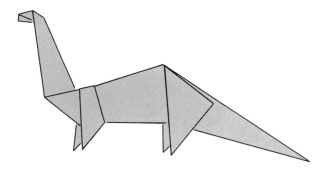

ANCHISAURUS

FOLDED SIZE: 7 1/8" **MATERIALS:** 2 sheets of 6" x 6" paper

Anchisaurus lived during the late Triassic period, over 180 million years ago. It was about two meters (6.5 feet) long, and may have eaten plants or meat. In the mid-nineteenth century, some of the first dinosaur bones found in North America included those of the *Anchisaurus*.

HEAD & UPPER BODY SECTION

STEP 1

Starting with **Fish Base** shown on page 10, valley fold diagonally folded edges of flaps to vertical center crease.

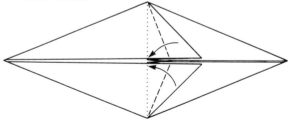

STEP 2

Mountain fold top edges of each triangle behind, one at a time.

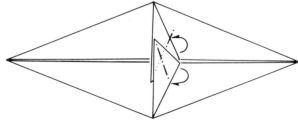

STEP 3

Turn over. Valley fold side edges to center line.

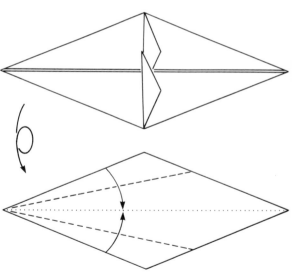

STEP 4

Valley fold model in half along center crease. Allow flaps formed in **Step 1** to swing free.

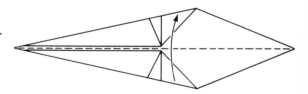

STEP 5

Inside reverse fold the neck up so that the back of the neck starts at a distance from the front of the leg equal to the width of the top of the leg.

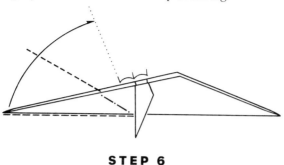

STEP 6

Inside reverse fold the head.

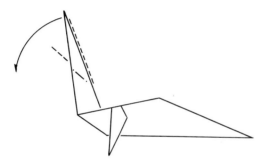

STEP 7

Pull out top layers. Pinch to define neck.

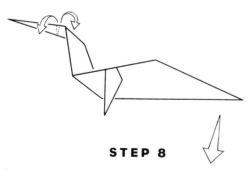

STEP 8

Shape.

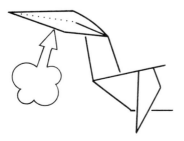

STEP 9

Inside reverse fold tip to form head.

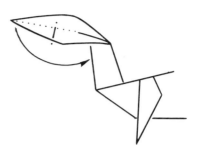

STEP 10

Inside reverse fold tip to form lower jaw.

STEP 11

Mountain fold corners inside to shape head. The **Head and Upper Body Section** is now finished, and you are ready to make the **Body and Tail Section.**

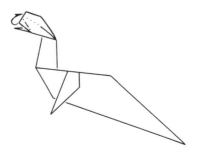

BODY & TAIL SECTION

With second sheet of paper, repeat **Steps 1,2,3, and 4** of the **Fish Base** on p. 10.

STEP 12

Valley fold flaps inward as shown, bringing ● to ○.

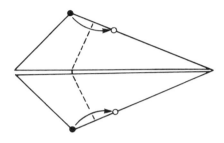

STEP 13

Turn over. Lift top flap and valley fold to left.

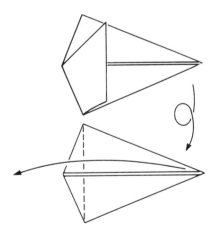

STEP 14

Valley fold tip to center.

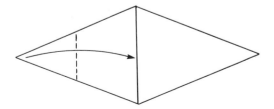

STEP 15

Valley fold in half along center line, allowing legs to swing free.

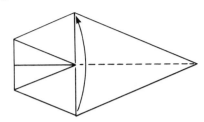

STEP 16

The **Body and Tail Section** is now finished. Insert the back tip of the **Upper Body Section** into it until the **Body and Tail Section** slides under the front legs.

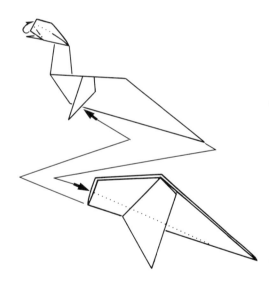

STEP 17

The model is now complete.

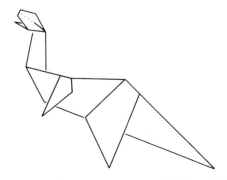

ALLOSAURUS

FOLDED SIZE: 6 1/2"   **MATERIALS:** 2 sheets of 6" by 6" paper; fine florist's wire

The *Allosaurus*, a carnivorous dinosaur that lived 140 million years ago, had teeth so sharp that some of their marks have been discovered on the bones of an *Apatosaurus*. The *Allosaurus* was ten meters (thirty-three feet) long and weighed two tons. The front legs of the *Allosaurus* were small, with sharp claws, but the rear legs were much longer, suggesting that it walked in an upright way.

HEAD & UPPER BODY SECTION

STEP 1

Starting with **Fish Base** shown on p.10, mountain fold diagonally folded edges of flaps to vertical center crease.

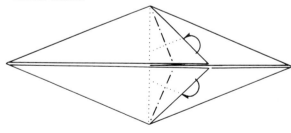

STEP 2

Valley fold lower flap in half to vertical center crease.

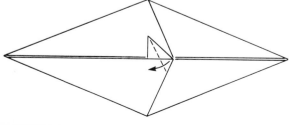

STEP 3

Repeat **Step 2** on other flap.

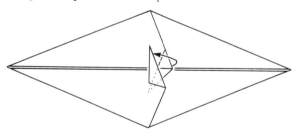

STEP 4

Turn over. Valley fold side edges to center line.

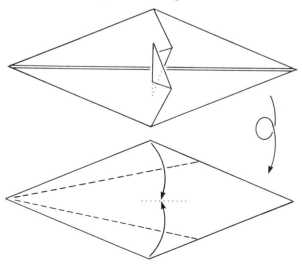

STEP 5

Valley fold model in half along center crease. Allow flaps to swing free.

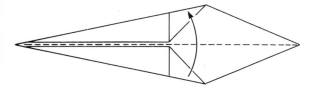

STEP 6

Check your orientation by comparing leg in diagram. Inside reverse fold the neck up.

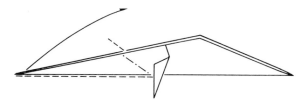

STEP 7

Inside reverse fold to make the head.

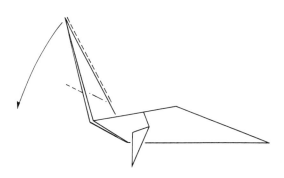

STEP 8

Pull out top layers and reform on existing creases. Pinch to define neck. The shape will be three-dimensional.

STEP 9

Inside reverse fold and pinch to form the nose.

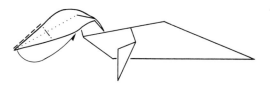

STEP 10

Inside reverse fold to form lower jaw.

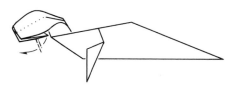

STEP 11

Tuck.

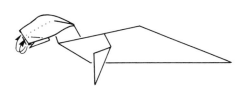

The **Head and Upper Body Section** is now finished, and you are ready to make the **Body and Tail Section.**

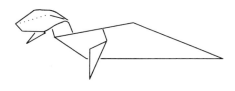

BODY & TAIL SECTION

The lower half of the body is made in the same way as that of the *Anchisaurus* (see p.27).

STEP 12

Join the two halves of the dinosaur together.

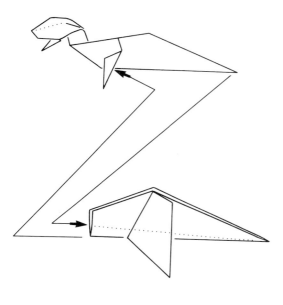

STEP 13

For added strength and flexibility, insert florist's wire in body. Shape the head.

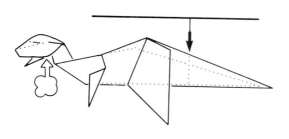

STEP 14

Curl the tail so that the model will stand erect.

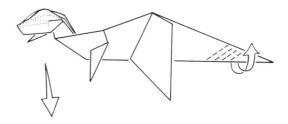

STEP 15

The advanced folder may add final touches to the head: Pinch to make ridges in center of head. Use a small outside reverse fold for the lower jaw.

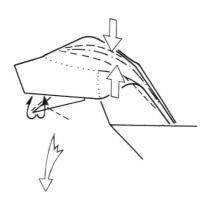

STEP 16

The model is now complete.

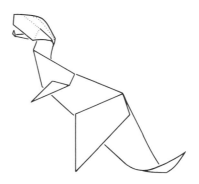

DIPLODOCUS

FOLDED SIZE: 9"   **MATERIALS:** 2 sheets of 6" x 6" paper

A gigantic plant-eating dinosaur of the late Jurassic period, *Diplodocus* was as long as twenty-seven meters (ninety feet) and weighed up to twelve tons; its shape was thinner than that of the *Apatosaurus*. *Diplodocus* lived 140 million years ago. Researchers now think these animals lived on land, rather than in the water, as was formerly believed.

HEAD & UPPER BODY SECTION

STEP 1

Starting with **Fish Base** shown on p.10, valley fold diagonally folded edges of flaps to vertical center crease and unfold to make landmark creases.

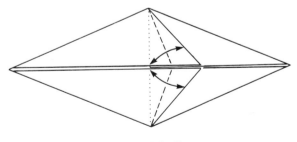

STEP 2

Valley fold tips to landmark creases.

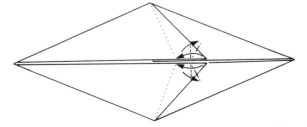

STEP 2A

Valley fold both tips back up at a slight angle.

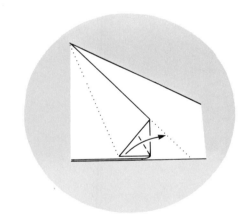

STEP 3

Valley fold both flaps down along creases made in **Step 1**.

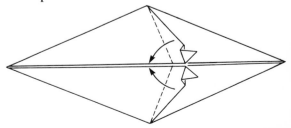

STEP 4

Turn over. Valley fold side edges to center line.

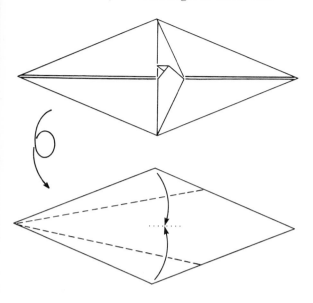

STEP 5

Valley fold model in half along center crease. Allow flaps to swing free.

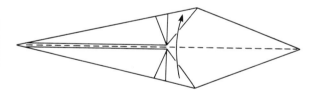

STEP 6

Orient the model. Inside reverse fold the neck up. The back of the neck should start at twice the width of the leg.

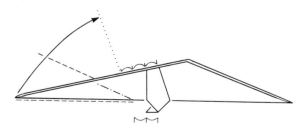

STEP 7

Starting 1/3 of the way down the back of the neck, inside reverse fold the head.

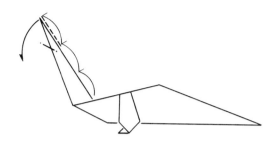

STEP 8

Outside reverse fold tip of head to touch front of neck. The **Head and Upper Body Section** is now finished, and you are ready to make the **Body and Tail Section**.

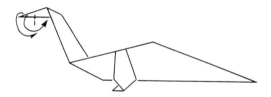

▼▼▼ BODY & TAIL ▼▼▼ SECTION

STEP 9

Starting with Step 7 of the *Apatosaurus* **Body and Tail Section** on p. 19, rotate the model to the left. Mountain fold the tips on both sides.

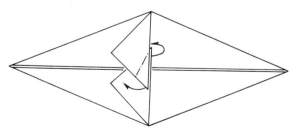

STEP 10

The base of the foot will be parallel to the center line. Turn over.

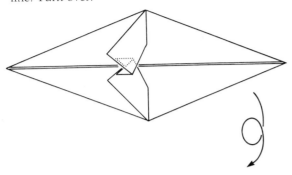

STEP 11

Valley fold side edges to center line. Valley fold the left tip to the point indicated.

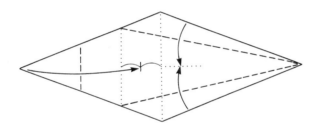

STEP 12

Valley fold model in half along center crease. Allow flaps to swing free.

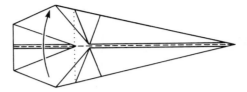

STEP 13

The **Body and Tail Section** is now finished. Join the **Head and Upper Body Section** to it (see p.20).

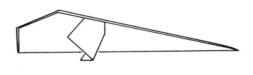

STEP 14

Crimp to lower the tail. The model is now complete.

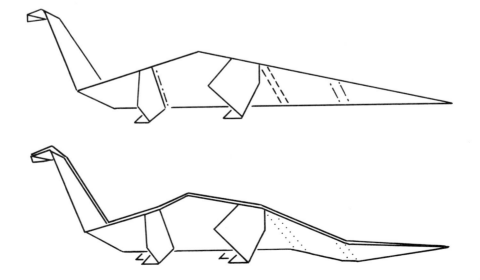

EDMONTOSAURUS

FOLDED SIZE: 7 1/2" MATERIALS: 2 sheets of 6" x 6" paper

The *Edmontosaurus* (*Trachodon*) was twelve meters (forty feet) long. This dinosaur was a hadrosaur—a duckbilled dinosaur. A plant-eater, its jaws held two thousand small teeth. Many species related to the *Edmontosaurus*, all of them with webbed feet, have been discovered. They lived around seventy million years ago.

HEAD & UPPER BODY SECTION

STEP 1

Starting with **Fish Base** shown on p. 10, fold the small triangles to the outside.

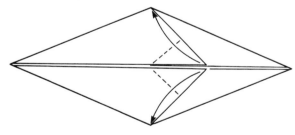

STEP 2

Pre-crease first, and then inside reverse fold.

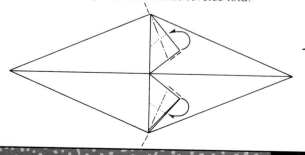

STEP 3

Turn over. Valley fold to center point.

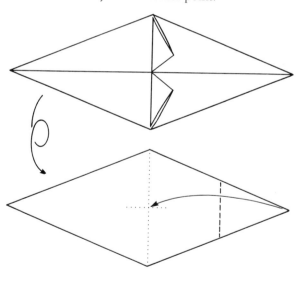

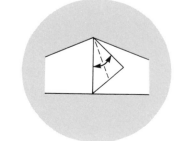

STEP 4

Valley fold side edges to center line.

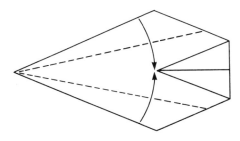

STEP 5

Valley fold as indicated by arrows.

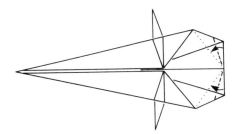

STEP 6

Turn over. Valley fold in half.

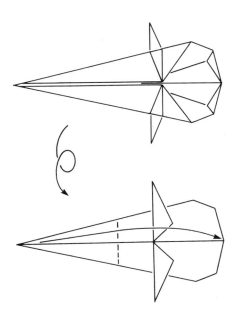

STEP 7

Valley fold top flap to the left so that the fold line aligns with legs.

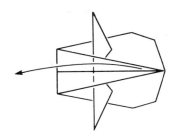

STEP 8

Mountain fold tip behind.

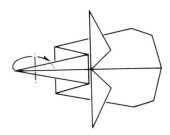

STEP 9

Mountain fold model in half.

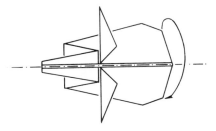

STEP 10

Pull the top layer up and create fold along indicated line.

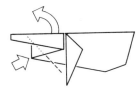

STEP 11

Pull head up and create fold along indicated line.

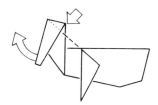

STEP 12

Pull out inside layers from beneath head and reform along fold line formed in **Step 7**. Shape duckbill.

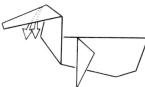

STEP 13

Open body to prepare it to be joined with the tail section.

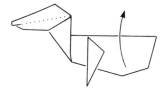

▾▾▾ BODY & TAIL ▾▾▾
SECTION

STEP 14

With second sheet of paper, fold through **Step 14** of *Anchisaurus* on p. 23. Turn over.

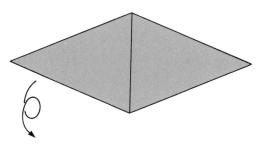

STEP 14A

Pull out top flap.

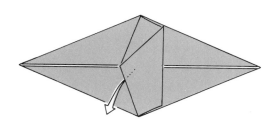

STEP 15

Close. Shift layer to the inside as the flap is flattened.

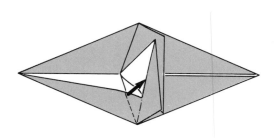

STEP 16

Pull out top layer.

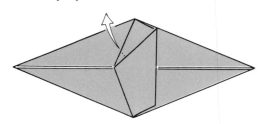

STEP 16A

Close. This repeats **Steps 14A** and **15** on the other side.

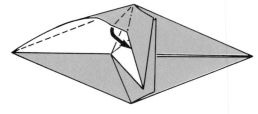

STEP 17

Orient the model. Mountain fold model in half, allowing legs to swing free.

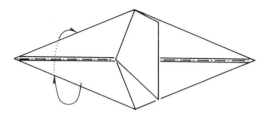

STEP 18

At the mid-point of the front half, inside reverse fold up.

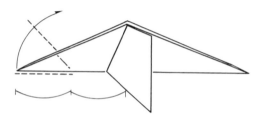

STEP 19

Inside reverse fold head as shown.

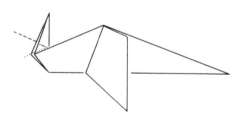

STEP 20

Fold far flap down.

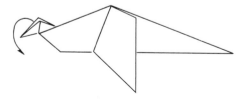

STEP 21

The **Body and Tail Section** is now finished, and you are ready to join the **Head and Upper Body Section** to it.

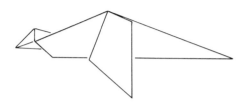

JOINING THE SECTIONS TOGETHER

STEP 22

Insert the tip of the tail section centrally in between the layers of the **Upper Section**. This is a very secure lock. Note that the back end of the head section touches the top of the rear legs.

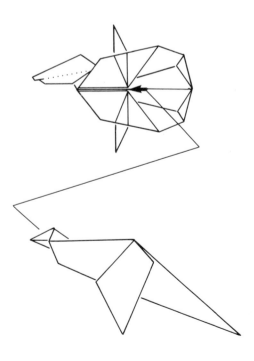

STEP 23

Close body, inserting flap behind leg.

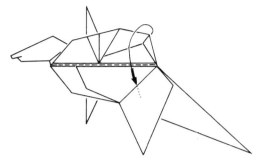

Turn over.

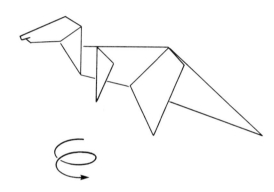

STEP 24

Lift up the flap of the leg.

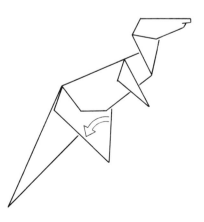

STEP 25

Tuck the back of the **Upper Body Section** inside and close.

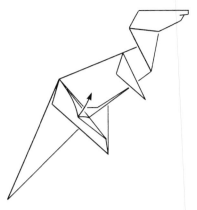

STEP 26

Add details: Roll up tail. On front legs, crimp to form small hands. You may tuck the head in just behind the duckbill to further shape it.

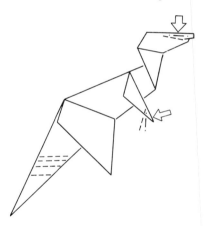

STEP 27

The model is now complete.

PARASAUROLOPHUS

FOLDED SIZE: 6 1/2"   **MATERIALS:** 2 sheets of 6" x 6" paper

The duckbilled mouth, webbed feet, and skeleton of this thirty-foot-long dinosaur relate it to the *Edmontosaurus* —it too was a hadrosaur. The name *Parasaurolophus* translates as "reptile with parallel-sided crest." This refers to the animal's long tubular crest, which curved back from its snout for a distance of up to 6 feet (1.8 m). *Parasaurolophus* lived sixty-eight million years ago, in the late Cretaceous period.

▼▼▼▼▼▼▼ HEAD & ▼▼▼▼▼▼▼ UPPER BODY SECTION

STEP 1

Fold through **Step 4** of **Fish Base**, p. 10. Valley fold flaps to high points of triangles.

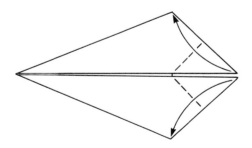

STEP 2

Inside reverse fold along creases on each side.

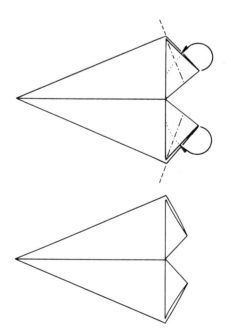

STEP 3

Turn over. Valley fold side edges to center line.

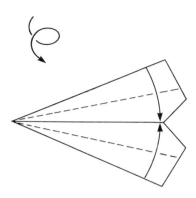

STEP 4

Valley fold model in half.

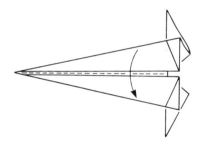

STEP 5

Outside reverse fold the neck up. Note where back of neck ends.

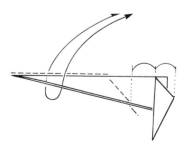

STEP 6

Outside reverse fold to form the head.

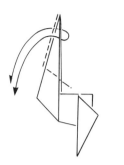

STEP 7

Pull out inside layers of the head.

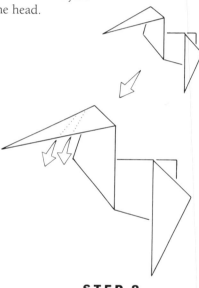

STEP 8

Pull top layer to an outside reverse fold to the rear.

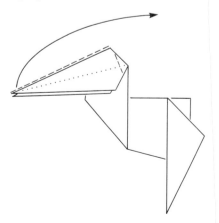

STEP 9

You have now formed the crest. Carefully, pull out its inside flaps. This step takes care and patience.

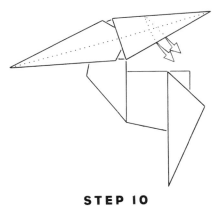

STEP 12

Make the **Body and Tail Section** as for the *Edmontosaurus*, through **Step 17** (p. 32-33). Slide **Body and Tail Section** into **Upper Body Section** and close.

STEP 10

Inside reverse fold the tip of the nose.

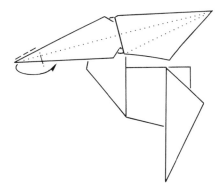

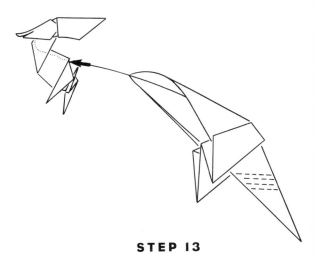

STEP 11

Pinch to make small crimps on both sides of the nose to shape it. Push and shape the crest.

STEP 13

The model is now complete.

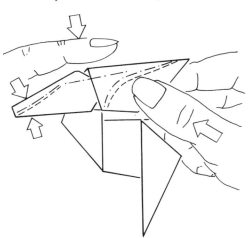

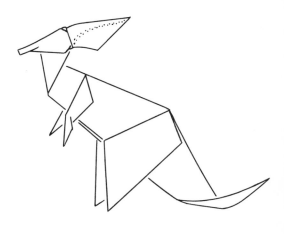

STEGOSAURUS

FOLDED SIZE: 6 1/2"   **MATERIALS:** Two sheets of 6" x 6" paper, with a 3" x 12" strip of paper for making the plates on the back

The most striking feature of the *Stegosaurus* is the double file of bone plates upon its back, arranged in an alternating pattern. The *Stegosaurus* had sharp spikes at the end of its tail. It lived around 140 million years ago, was ten meters (thirty-three feet) long, and weighed two tons. It was most likely a plant-eater, judging by the structure of its teeth and mouth.

HEAD & UPPER BODY SECTION

STEP 1

Starting with **Fish Base** shown on p. 10, valley fold diagonally folded edges of flaps to vertical center crease.

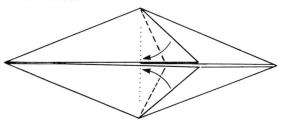

BODY & TAIL SECTION

STEP 2

Starting with **Fish Base** shown on p. 10, mountain fold behind. Note where tip lies.

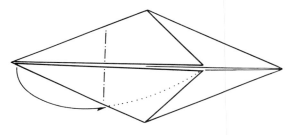

STEP 3

Valley fold diagonally folded edges of flaps to vertical center crease.

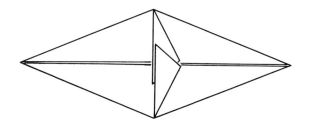

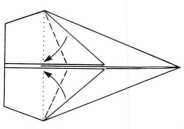

STEP 4

Pull flap to left. Reverse valley fold to mountain fold along each leg and flatten.

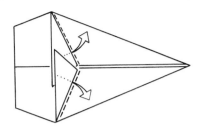

JOINING THE TWO SECTIONS AND CONTINUING

STEP 5

Connect **Head and Upper Body Section** to **Body and Tail Section** by inserting **Body and Tail Section** under the small flaps.

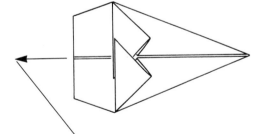

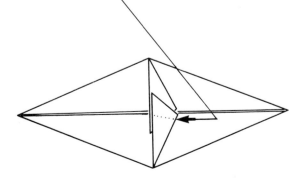

STEP 6

Mountain fold edges behind.

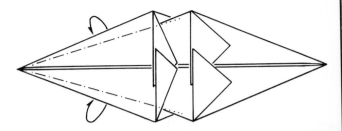

STEP 7

Carefully noting the distance indicated in the diagram, valley fold point to the right.

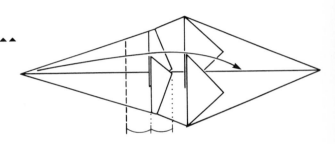

STEP 8

Using base of legs as fold line, fold flap to left.

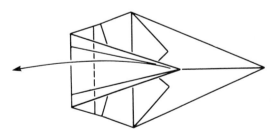

Turn over.

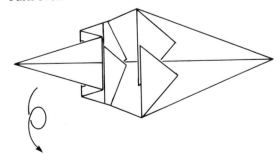

STEP 9

Note outline of lower layer flap. Mountain fold both layers of the **Head and Upper Body Section** behind and tuck.

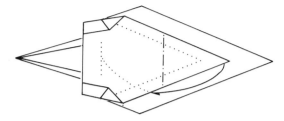

This locks the pieces together, giving you this cross-section:

STEP 10

Valley fold the model in half, allowing legs to swing free.

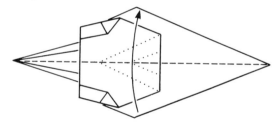

STEP 11

Pull.

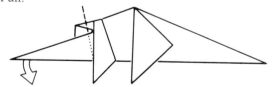

STEP 12

Inside reverse fold the neck up.

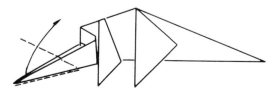

STEP 13

Inside reverse fold to form the head.

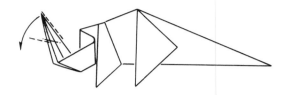

STEP 14

Pull out the top layer from inside the head and reform on existing creases.

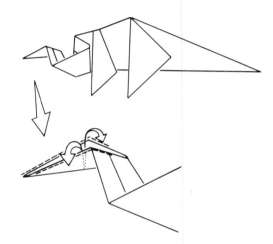

STEP 15

Shape the head.

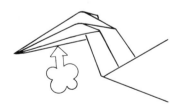

STEP 16

Inside reverse fold.

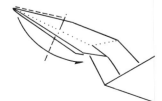

STEP 17

Inside reverse fold to form lower jaw.

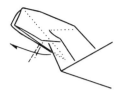

STEP 18

Mountain fold both sides of upper jaw inside.

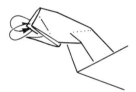

STEP 19

Shape the head.

STEP 20

Starting at the base of the tail and ending 3/4 of the way down the back of the tail, inside reverse fold.

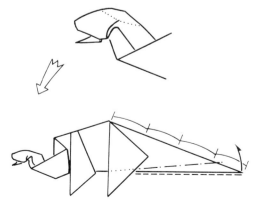

STEP 21

Close-up of tail: inside reverse fold.

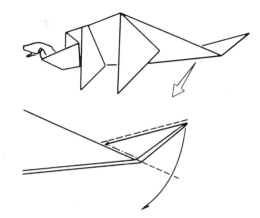

STEP 22

Inside reverse fold.

STEP 23

Inside reverse fold.

STEP 24

Inside reverse fold.

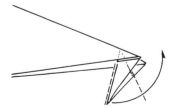

STEP 25

Inside reverse fold on both sides.

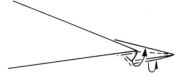 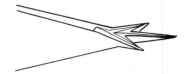

The upper and lower sections of the model have now been completed, and you are ready to make the plates.

MAKING THE PLATES FOR THE BACK

STEP 26

Using a 3" x 12" strip of paper, valley fold side edges to center crease.

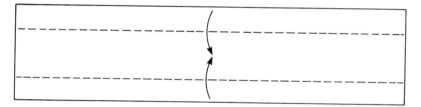

STEP 27

Make a mountain fold at the halfway point and then at the 1/4 and 3/4 points; unfold.

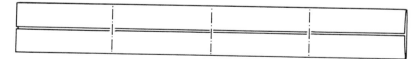

STEP 28

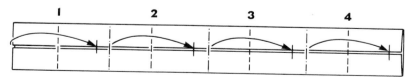

1. Valley fold edge almost to mountain crease.
2. Fold mountain crease almost to next mountain crease.
3. Repeat **Step 2**.
4. Repeat almost to end.

STEP 29

Mountain fold in half.

STEP 30

Pull and pivot each plate.

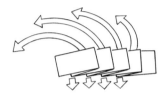

STEP 31

Valley fold alternate flaps down. Turn over.
Again valley fold alternate flaps down. Turn over.

STEP 32

Alternately mountain and valley fold flaps
backward and forward to separate plates.

STEP 33

Plates finished:

Top view:

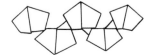

STEP 34

Insert the plates in back.

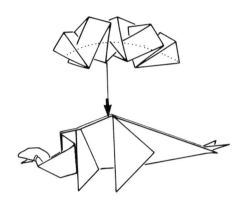

STEP 35

Outside crimp tail. (See *Crimp*, p. 8.)

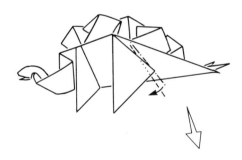

STEP 36

The model is now complete.

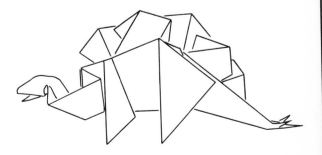

TYRANNOSAURUS

FOLDED SIZE: 5 1/8" **MATERIALS:** One sheet of 6" x 6" paper

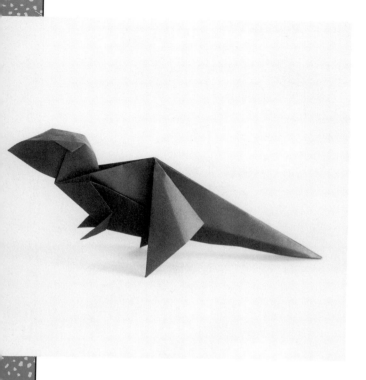

One of a group of dinosaurs that first appeared 130 million years ago during the Cretaceous period and became extinct 65 million years ago, the *Tyrannosaurus* itself lived toward the end of this period. A gigantic meat-eater, this dinosaur was thirteen meters (forty-two feet) long and weighed seven tons. In its great mouth were many teeth as sharp as knives. Because the front legs were relatively small, the *Tyrannosaurus* is believed to have walked upright.

STEP 1

White side up, book fold both sides. Valley fold adjacent corners to the center, one set in front and one behind.

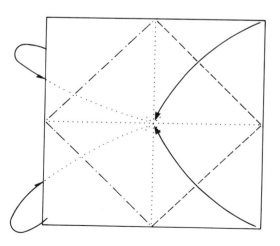

STEP 2

Proceed to make a **Fish Base** from this same paper. To do so, turn to p.10 and begin from **Step 1**.

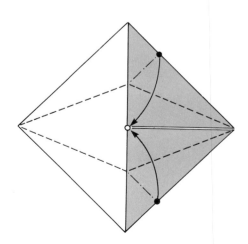

STEP 3

Open out the white flaps on the far side, making a square.

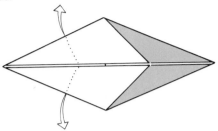

STEP 4

Using the square, make a **Fish Base** (see p. 10).

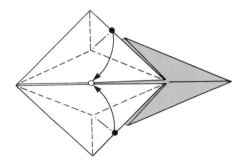

STEP 5

Valley fold diagonally folded edges of flaps to vertical center crease.

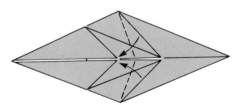

STEP 6

Pull flap to left. Reverse valley fold to mountain fold along each leg and flatten.

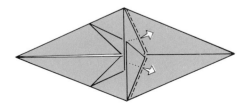

STEP 7

Valley fold the small flaps to the indicated line.

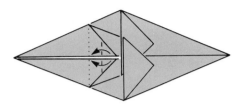

STEP 8

Mountain fold the model in half, allowing the legs to swing free.

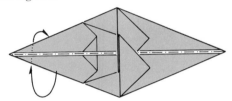

STEP 9

Inside reverse fold the neck up.

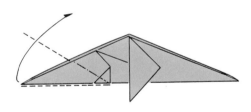

STEP 10

Inside reverse fold the head down.

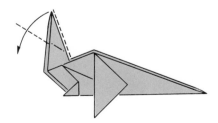

STEP 11

Valley fold down both sides of the head.

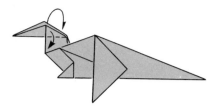

STEP 12

Unfold and lift the top layer only. The inside flap remains as is (see close-up). Repeat on other side.

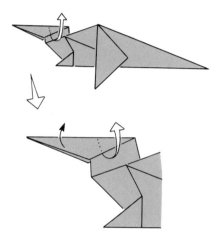

STEP 13

Valley fold down a small triangle to round the head (see close-up). Repeat on other side.

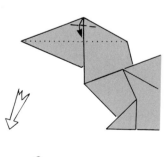

STEP 14

Stretch and shape the head.

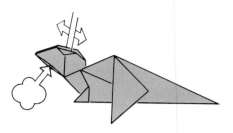

STEP 15

Push in on either side of the tail to shape the body and make the dinosaur three-dimensional.

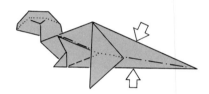

STEP 16

The model is now complete. Stand it on its rear legs.

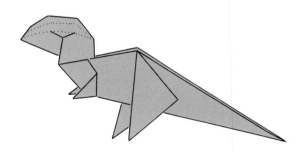

DIMETRODON

FOLDED SIZE: 5"   **MATERIALS:** One sheet of 6" x 6" paper

The *Dimetrodon* had a dorsal fin that looked like a sail. This creature was four meters (thirteen feet) long. It lived in the marshes 275 million years ago during the Permian period, prior to the age of dinosaurs. Many different kinds of animals lived on earth then.

STEP 1

Starting with the **Primitive Base** shown on p. 15, swing leg back on its natural hinge.

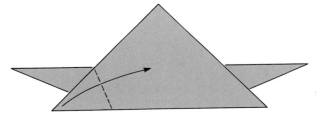

STEP 2

Crimp on both sides to form head.

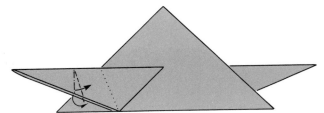

STEP 3

Inside reverse fold tip to define nose.

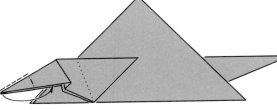

STEP 4

Valley fold leg down to match crease formed by hinge.

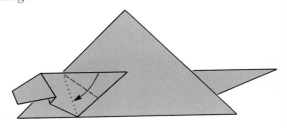

Repeat **Steps 1** and **4** on other side to form the other leg.

STEP 5

Valley fold up as shown.

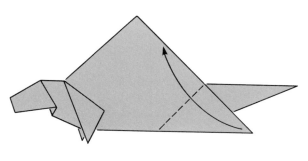

STEP 6

Make creases and flatten tail down on both sides, while also folding down legs.

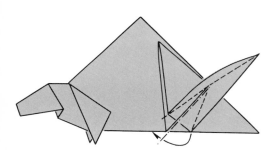

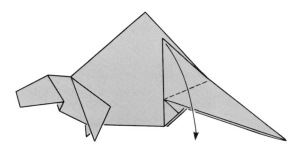

STEP 7

Mountain fold and tuck one dorsal fin inside. Mountain fold and shape the neck and belly as shown. Make tuck at base of model as shown.

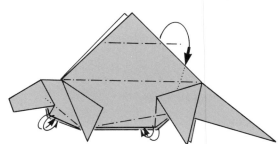

STEP 8

Make creases only on the dorsal fin. The model is now complete.

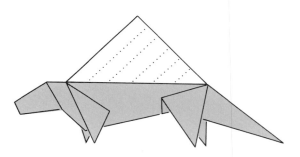

PTERANODON

FOLDED SIZE: 6 3/4"   **MATERIALS:** One sheet of 6" x 6" paper

This model can really fly! It is the *Pteranodon*, a pterosaur that lived seventy million years ago. Its wings were eight meters (twenty-six feet) across when spread—big enough to span a two-lane highway. If you suspend some *Pteranodon* and *Rhamphorhyncus* (p. 52), you can make a prehistoric mobile.

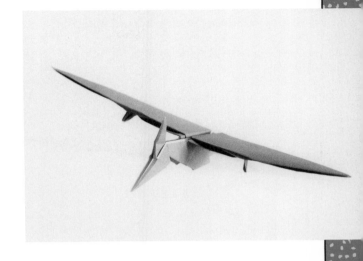

STEP 1

Make a center landmark crease. Valley fold to the right.

STEP 2

Valley fold base to tip of triangle.

STEP 3

Valley fold, leaving tip of triangle free. Unfold, returning to shape seen in **Step 2**.

STEP 4

Bring mountain fold line marked ● to the crease marked ○ and then fold.

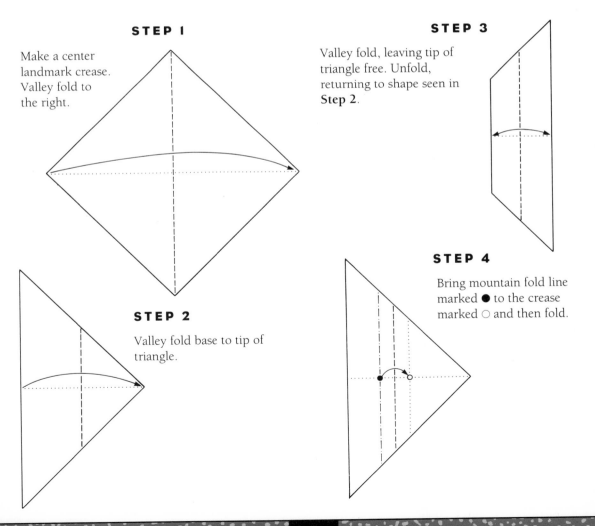

STEP 5

Bring corner ● to ○ and fold.

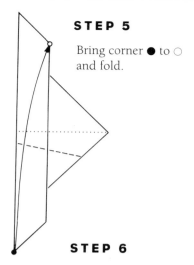

STEP 6

Mountain fold model in half along diagonal crease.

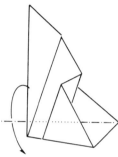

STEP 7

Mountain fold lower flap behind to match other flap.

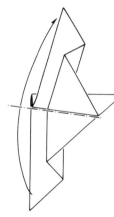

STEP 8

Valley fold flap up to match folded edge.

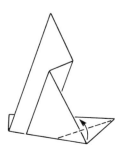

STEP 9

Valley fold flap back.

STEP 10

Inside reverse fold.

STEP 11

Inside reverse fold.

STEP 12

Valley fold. Crimp where indicated.

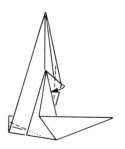

Repeat **Steps 8** to **12** on other side.

STEP 13

Outside reverse fold.

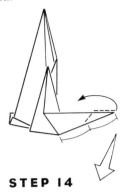

STEP 14

Pull out the inside flaps.

STEP 15

On both sides, valley fold flaps to the outside.

STEP 16

Unfold only the top layer back to the shape seen in **Step 13**.

STEP 17

Crimp on both sides.

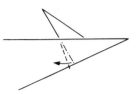

STEP 18

Tuck on both sides.

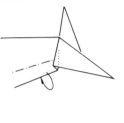

STEP 19

Valley fold wings down on both sides, forming right angles.

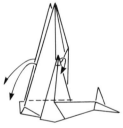

STEP 20

The model is now complete. Fly it!

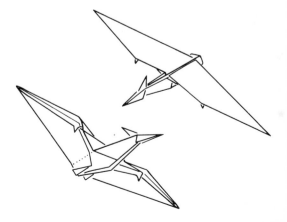

RHAMPHORHYNCUS

FOLDED SIZE: 5 1/8" wingspan **MATERIALS:** One sheet of 6" x 6" paper

The *Rhamphorhyncus*, which lived 140 million years ago, had a wingspan of eighty centimeters (thirty-two inches). The tip of its long tail had a fan. This creature was an early pterosaur, which means "winged lizard."

STEP 1

Starting with the **Bird Base** on p. 13, make crease lines as indicated. Push crease inside, bringing the ● to the ○ on the inside.

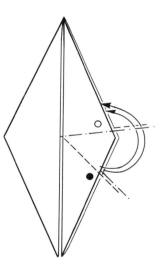

STEP 2

Inside reverse fold.
Outside reverse fold.

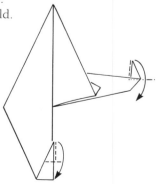

STEP 3

Inside reverse fold.
Outside reverse fold.

STEP 4

Pull out inside reverse fold made in **Step 3** and open up inside layers.

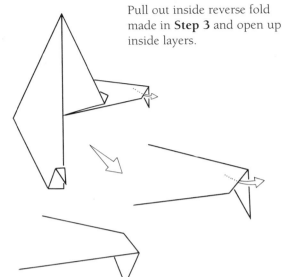

STEP 5

Valley fold up on both sides.

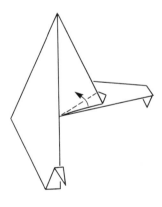

STEP 6

Inside reverse fold down on both sides.

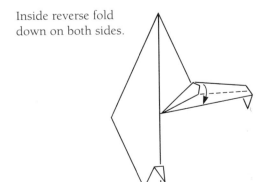

STEP 7

Valley fold forward on both sides.

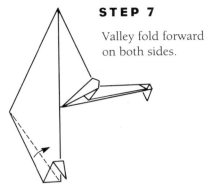

STEP 8

Valley fold forward on both sides.

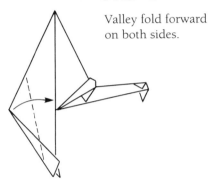

STEP 9

Valley fold forward on both sides.

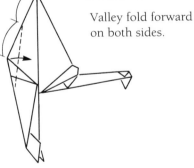

STEP 10

Unfold top layer only.

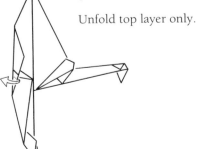

STEP 11

Trim edges by valley folding. Inside reverse fold as indicated.

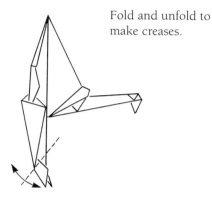

STEP 12

Fold and unfold to make creases.

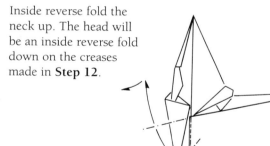

STEP 13

Inside reverse fold the neck up. The head will be an inside reverse fold down on the creases made in **Step 12**.

STEP 14

Fold down the wings, forming right angles.

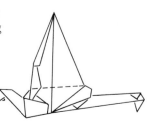

STEP 15

Valley fold and tuck flap inside.

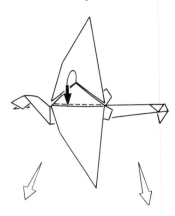

STEP 16

A. Valley fold on both sides. Shape head.
B. Valley fold on both sides to lift and open up tail.

A   **B**

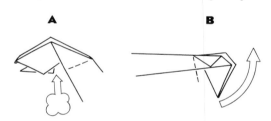

STEP 17

The model is now complete. It can really fly!

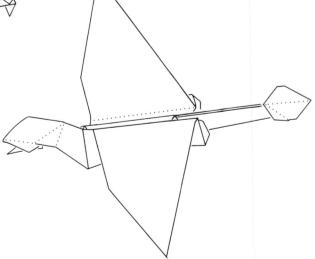

IGUANODON

FOLDED SIZE: 6 3/4"   **MATERIALS:** 2 sheets of 6" x 6" paper

The teeth of the first dinosaur discovered were those of the *Iguanodon*. The name comes from the Iguana, whose teeth are in fact quite similar. The plant-eating *Iguanodon* lived 135 million years ago, was eight meters (twenty-six feet) long, weighed four-and-a-half tons, and walked in an upright way.

HEAD & UPPER BODY SECTION

STEP 1

Starting with the **Bird Base** on p.13, valley fold one flap down.

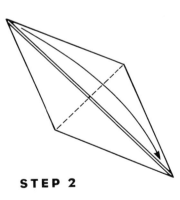

STEP 2

Valley fold triangular flap down.

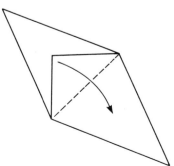

STEP 3

Valley fold model in half.

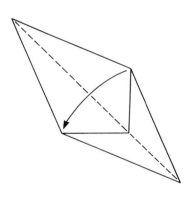

STEP 4

Pull up on middle flap. Angle and flatten.

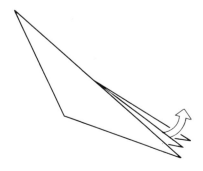

STEP 5

Inside reverse fold. Tuck.

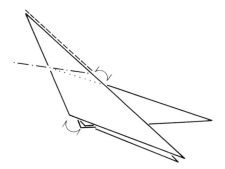

STEP 6

Outside reverse fold.

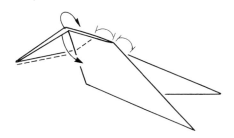

STEP 7

Inside reverse fold.

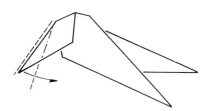

STEP 8

Inside reverse fold.

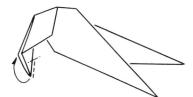

STEP 9

Inside reverse fold to tuck the arrowed section.

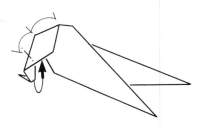

STEP 10

Mountain fold edges to tuck inside.

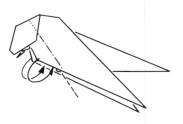

STEP 11

Inside reverse fold both front legs.

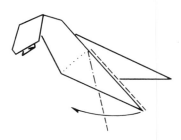

STEP 12

Inside reverse fold on both sides.

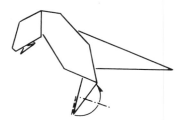

STEP 13

Make a simple valley fold of inner triangle only.

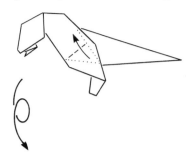

View from underneath:

▼▼▼ **BODY & TAIL SECTION** ▼▼▼

STEP 14

With second sheet of paper, repeat through **Step 2** above. Turn over. Make simple valley folds to the crease on both sides.

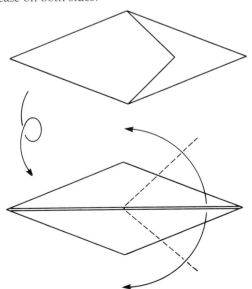

STEP 15

Pull up on leg. Lift as indicated. Shift layers to the inside of the leg (see detail). Repeat on other leg.

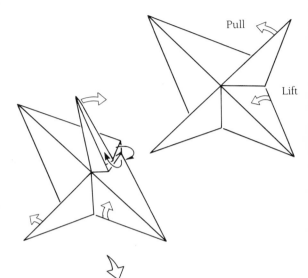

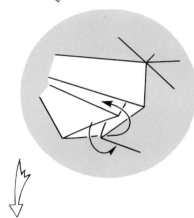

STEP 16

Inside reverse fold and repeat on other leg.

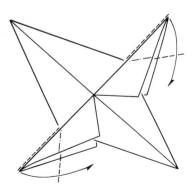

STEP 17

Make inside reverse folds on each leg to form the feet.

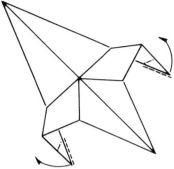

STEP 19

Valley fold edges of the body only toward the center. Note fold continues beneath legs.

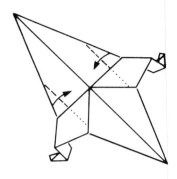

STEP 18

Outside reverse fold tips.

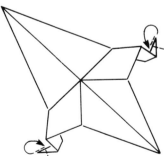

STEP 20

Thin tail by mountain folding a small bit behind.

STEP 21

Watch creases on both sides carefully as you pinch as indicated. Open up inner layers and shape the body into three dimensions. Turn over.

Top:

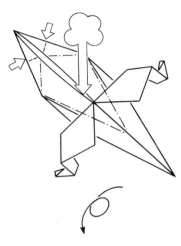

Bottom: Pinch as indicated.

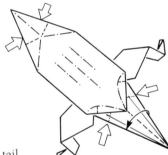

Valley fold tail.

STEP 22

Inside reverse fold.

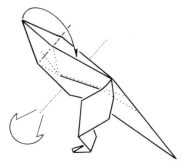

▼▼▼ JOINING THE ▼▼▼ TWO SECTIONS
▲▲▲▲▲▲▲▲▲▲▲▲▲▲▲▲▲▲▲▲▲▲▲▲▲

STEP 23

The **Body and Tail Section** is now finished. Shape the head on the **Head and Upper Body Section**. Join the two sections.

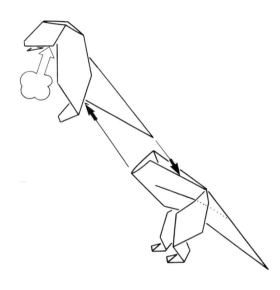

STEP 24

The model is now complete.

GODZILLA

FOLDED SIZE: 6 1/2" **MATERIALS:** 2 sheets of 6" x 6" paper, with a 1" x 6" strip of paper for making the dorsal fin; fine florist's wire

Godzilla is the monster made famous by the science-fiction films of the same title, the first of which was made in Japan in 1954. The figure of Godzilla was based upon the *Iguanodon*. The name combines "Go-Ri-Ra" (Gorilla) with "Ku-Zi-Ra" (Whale). In the film, Godzilla is awakened by the explosion of an atomic bomb and arises from the sea to attack Japan. The movie was a great success in Japan and contributed to the antinuclear movement there.

When making this model, keep checking your orientation and keep looking ahead to the next diagram to make sure the folding is exact.

STEP 1

To make the **Body and Tail Section**, fold through **Step 16** of the *Iguanodon* on p. 58. Crimp on side on both legs.

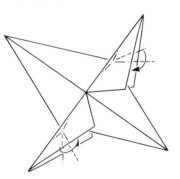

STEP 2

Inside reverse fold on both sides.

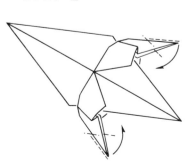

STEP 3

Inside reverse fold on both sides.

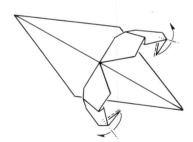

STEP 4

Fold the **Head and Upper Body Section** of the *Iguanodon* on pp. 55-57. Join the two sections together.

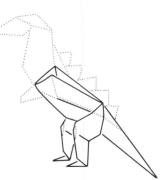

THE DORSAL FIN

STEP 5

Using a 1" x 6" strip of paper, measure intervals of 5/8" (1.5 cm.) and mark. Starting on the right, valley fold and then proceed to alternately mountain and valley fold as indicated.

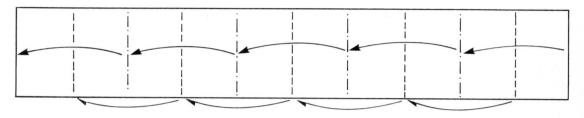

STEP 6

Make creases as indicated.

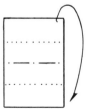

STEP 7

Mountain fold behind.

STEP 8

Inside reverse fold.

STEP 9

Valley fold up.

STEP 10

Mountain fold as indicated.

STEP 11

Pull out accordian-style.

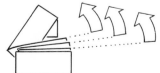

STEP 12

Pull each segment out as indicated.

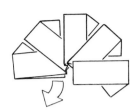

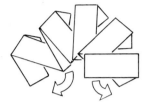

STEP 13

Valley fold each segment down.

STEP 14

Mountain fold each segment behind.

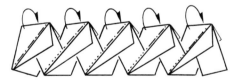

STEP 15

Open and squash fold on lower portion, continuing until the end of the strip.

STEP 16

Close the squash folds.

STEP 17

Insert into dorsal cleft (the opening in the back). Insert florist's wire into body (see **Step 13** on p. 26), shaping the tail.

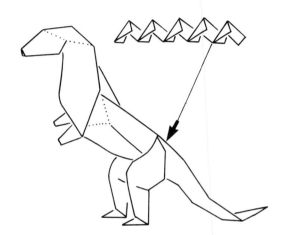

STEP 18

The model is now complete.

ORNITHOLESTES

FOLDED SIZE: 5 1/8"   **MATERIALS:** One sheet of 6" x 6" paper

Ornitholestes lived 140 million years ago. A small meat-eater, it was about the same height as a person. The bones of this dinosaur were discovered in Wyoming.

STEP 1

Starting with the **Bird Base** on p. 13, make a simple mountain fold.

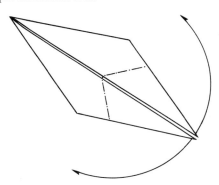

STEP 2

Inside reverse fold on both sides.

STEP 3

Valley fold the front flap only.

STEP 4

Valley fold the model in half.

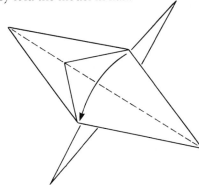

STEP 5

Cut as indicated and then outside reverse fold.

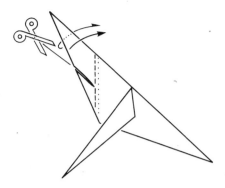

STEP 7

Outside reverse fold once to create head. Outside reverse fold each leg twice to create knees and feet.

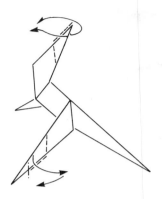

STEP 6

Mountain fold on both sides and tuck in.

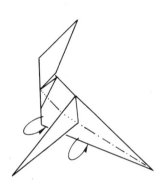

STEP 8

The model is now complete.

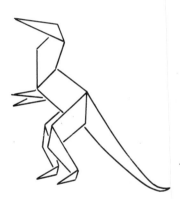

Origami paper can be found in many arts-and-crafts stores and in some museum shops and Japanese bookstores.

Another mail-order source is The Friends of the Origami Center of America, 15 West 77th Street, New York, New York, 10024, (212) 769-5635.